planets,
gourds
and
traveling staffs
by
maya odim

breath is expansion.
this breath helps balance
it is the balance. it's the need transformed from selfish desire,
        past yearning to reality. this space. when you go ahead and
        do it you expand. this expansion helps you balance, it is the
        balance. it is the need transformed from selfish desire, past
        yearning to reality. this action, whatever you need it to be
have it be.
you have to be
the core of your peace
the life of your life, your story teller. i
really believe
freedom is what's within us. if we recognize what we feel is
        freedom and put that into practice we will always work to
        keep that a
constant.
we will be looking for those freedoms, always. that's why we can't
        tell people what makes them free- that's why we have to
        listen to them about their freedoms. people can try and take
        your freedom, you can make sure you remain free. no one
        can give you freedom. freedom can be rooted in the peace-
        fulness of strength. freedom is rooted in community.

hate is not free because hate is rooted in bondage. bondage means,
     not free to move
or change – bound to one position.
when we have decided to believe
what we hate only means these things that make us hate it,
we have bound what we hate
to only mean
deserving of hate.
we have bound ourselves to hating. when we let what we feel we
     hate have more of a meaning than only having a negative
     importance for us, we free ourselves from our position of
     hate.
we free.
we free ourselves...we do not make anyone free but ourselves,
     we can support the freedom of others. we don't have to
     justify separating ourself from any one idea or any one
     human or group or love. we leave what does not fit us, we
     grow where our roots are nourished. we can respect others
     roots nourishing. we are not safe if we have identified the
     enemy/unsafe/nigger/alien. we are safe if we are not needing
     to look for someone to brand as enemy/unsafe/nigger or
     alien. we are free.
when we see ourselves as ourselves, continuously growing...falling
     and getting up...staying up and staying cool...rooting in our
     communities (peace love and respect), we are free. working
     to build is building to freedom. you can't build alone

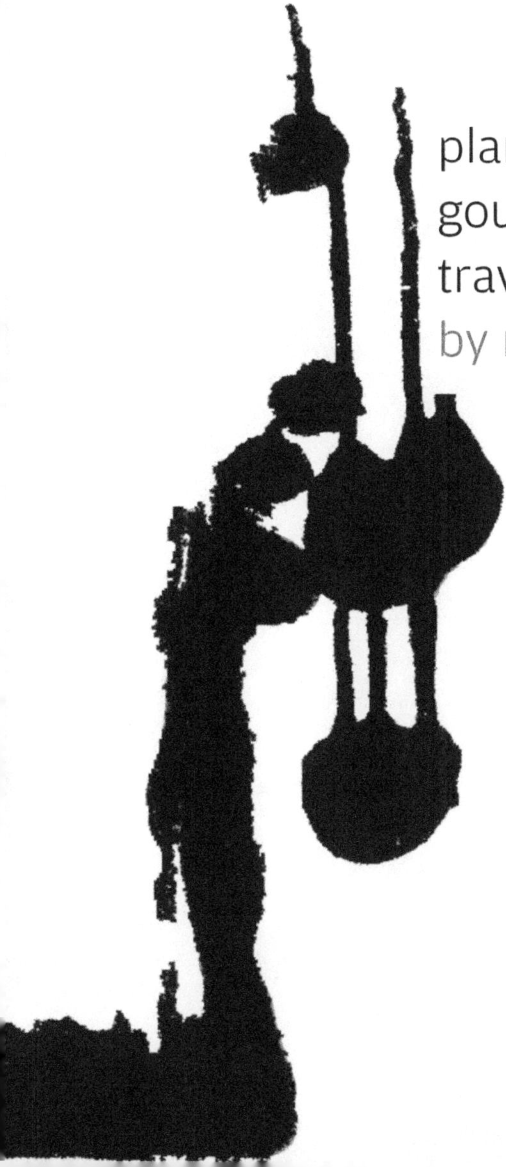

planets, gourds and traveling staffs

by maya odim

this book is dedicated to
my family

this book is dedicated to
my grandmothers,
Dorothy Elayne Jeffries
&
Emma Marie Cheek

Published in 2011 by Udala Press
P.O. Box 6303
Evanston, IL 60204
(312) 772-2396

ISBN: 978-0-9846866-0-5
Printed in the United States

Cover Art: Maya Odim
Cover & Interior Design: Greta Carlson

10 9 8 7 6 5 4 3 2 1

planets

all the time

speaking forward from where
    we come running
a gaggle of
where we come from,
running.

through the thickness that
    places itself forever in
    front of us
sometimes we dive, sometimes
    we push sometimes we
    pounce...always
regretting
sometimes.

even when we say we don't.

sprouting from the skins of
    our body we lay down
    the need
sprouting from our need
    we lay down the want
sprouting from the want
    we hold tight to wishes
night time, morning time,
    all the time, sometimes

story telling

for chaka and rashid

they've always said i talk white with my size ten feet and my
nigerian hips bouncing wildly north to cuban salsa's screaming
this black america (my body born into soil) the internal*isms* scar-
ing me into accepting what scars me because i think it's part of
the light, when it's not. wearing rings from mother's jewelry box
and knocking on solid wood mantels like they don't make them
anymore except for the ones on myrtle avenue. and knocking on
solid wood like my father every time he passes something put
together. looking towards my days with gray hair spinning gran-
ma's story from north carolina and warren county, jumbling my
words all into paragraphs of tobacco picking and worms in the
fields and raising fists Biafran-like not paying attention to what
the newspaper says about me. this is my prose piece for all of the
essays that didn't get me in... i'm in this with sore hip joints and
heavy memories maybe painlessly lifting their scars that leave
me wondering about what the point of scars aren't, which is to
leave a mark. that leaves me wondering when i will wonder no
more. knowing i will only do that once i stop wondering.

i talk "black" with my size ten feet and my nigerian hips
bouncing wildly north to cuban salsa's sharing this black ame-
rican (my body born into soil) screaming how i talk american!
telling this how i talk through the libations i'm leaving telling this
real loud, how if they try and stop ya from being you, get up and
be you somewhere else. oye?

this:

when you work on the core everything else falls into place,
don't need a structure to write a poem, don't need a template to
make life nice, don't even need these words to carry on, but ya
need the ones that came before them cause ya have to know where
ya came from to carry on

el arbol

this family is growing
continous looping
like birds grandmothers reincarnate into, swooping
circling, tracing pathways
leaving broken twigs along the trail,
the past days pathways for new babes
        to capture age
so they remember where their grandparents play.

this family is big blocks sturdy standing buildings
each of us, don't matter if we blood related
got our love to fill in

this family, we are women with strong necks and men
        with strong backs
we are women with strong backs and men with strong necks

family pedigree
hailing from the caspian sea
from cuban mambi waters and nigerian white and green and
        biafran freedom beams
from tobacco picking american soil and the sun's gleam

somos humanos
con corazónes palpitando
aquí estamos
creciendo porque dónde vamos
es dónde vamos.

contando las letras de como estamos

he oído de las ritmas oeste africanas palpitando en el parte atrás
de los dientes de mi mamá
mezclando con su cuba.

colores rojas que le guían por un par de tiempo
he oído de los musculos berceros contracting en las piernas
        de mi papá
palabras en cada corner que compartió pensamientos con él.
he oído de las letras de mi hermano dino
anudados
que en un coronamiento se quedaron en todas partes
        de su cabéza,
colores brias spraying alongside snap shots
queeeeee
reflected in his pupils

he oído del expresion libre en el parte atrás de la cabéza
        de mi hermano
chaka,
su espalda alargando al cielo.
algunas líneas derechas mostly curvas encima de

16

olas,
bebiendo.

he oído de esa familia
músculos saturados con colores
protegiendo pictures

al primer momento antes de que tomamos esa verdad...
y cuando lo bebemos
y cuanto bebemos
nadando el sistema
nadando mi sistema

bailando encima de las habichuelas
caminando alongside la pared fuera de la escuela,
dejando lo ir
se va se va volando la vida

gourds

cross roads

i've heard that punishment teaches,
    scares ya into not wrongin again.
punishment scars. stops ya from moving,
    doesn't teach ya at all,

ya gotta learn what needs to be done and what
    can wait to be done.

i've heard that losing somethin makes ya more
    careful...
to keep a better eye out,
loss does nothing but sow seeds of regret.
    ya gotta learn to let go.
i've heard that heart break makes us stronger...
    heart break can stop
the growth
but ya learn to keep growing

people talk about toughenin up, not being too
    nice, not sharing too much,
someone will take advantage of us!

...gotta continue talking bout what love helps
build, gotta uplift the trust to live. we have to be
strong. when will we tell ourselves we
have to care to not lose, telling ourselves our bad
days will knock us down and our good days will
build us up.
we are not these warriors made of metal hearts,
    we are these warriors
of skin and bone. these warriors who wail and
    moan, who live and grow
strong and weak.

waxing/waning

        just laid there and made noises
noises like the sound of CTA trains' brakes screeching,
noises that sounded of sorrow.
radiating from the stomach
faaar from the heart, faaar from the brain
very close to the tongue.

waves clap up loooud and hard! on lake michigan's shores
kinda sounds like the tongue clapping against teeeth,
saliva

nervousness
this feeling of nervousness is rooted in unhappiness
this feeling of unhappiness is rooted in the belief that the past
     could have been different
than it was,

this feeling of balance, of steadiness
can only be found once the belief is found that the past
      is as it doooes…
did.
no periods needed, doors closed
windows open

like they say the gods do.

how can the mind be so sure of something the body has yet
      to believe?
because, because we can reach past the finger tips
      and touch with energy
because life is not always about being prepared and ready
because truth is in action cause these people's words can deceive

coronas

wisk sparking
hefnr spacing
letting out *feers*
and using more colors, queens sprinkling from
      the skies rocking three pointed crowns.

with lower legs hanging
feet up, palms sometimes leaning
not covering the strength, piecing it.
not working to prove anything cause you can't
      work like that anyway
the stars light my path
draped in black i jump, into memory often

we are north now...

(one time towards the end you looked at me)
one time towards the end he looked at me and
      said sighing, thinking about weather
or not
to use his middle
"it's hard to let a pretty girl go."

just cause i didn't say it then doesn't mean
      don't speak it now, pretty?
i am a thinker lover laugher word gurl picture
      maker traveler
mover
daughter granddaughter younger sister aunt
      cousin, niece, huh
and pretty is what you
see...when our bodies came out of the phone
      the flood rushed in

u were wearing black and green and your hair
i was wearing green and blue
we were these friends as they come before
        relationships
and we left flowers everywhere, everywhere,
        everywhere
and i am still confused as to how to water them.

we are south of no north now,
with bukoswki and bobbie humphrey playing
        that flute singing fly bird
donald fly,
think twice think twice think twice,
        say it three times
so it sticks to the backs of plumb skinz
blacks and blues, manchas de la tierra
don't forget esa tierra (don't forget es la tierra)

professor

the unified positions of jazz musics, and mournings,
and light mornings are of:
that scratch, that hold
that thrust as a way of talking about
composite
synergies and states
with questions, interpreting what these questions mean
organizing their meanings
and giving a response
based on reality, or fantasy
hollering.

the part of the identity is this,
as how it comes in poetics
and clacking, clacking loud keys loudly

no more mourning.
getting caught sleeping on the mother city
waking up to the horns, scratching
holding, jazzing

that scratch
that hold
mourning lightly in poetics
and filling the bowl of every color blackness
the night time blackness
the green
the red liberation blackness heard in the musics

in these steps

always recognize the spirits, recognize who ya
     identify as family
and the ones who have already gone home.
recognize ya friends, too, here and at home.
gotta do this before it all, quiet and out loud.

a place right after:
go where ya feel good and feel good where ya go

a place after that:
eat well to keep spirit up
then into moons ya can imagine traveling,
     imagine traveling
and setting up home
living with enough
enough to spread
and your arms with space to roam
     and space to bring friends

spring

it's been raining for days
moist and cool in the air like this
for days

and feeling good, knowing footing wise
        grandmothers smell lingering in the air too.
been feeling just ripe thought burning my lips
chilies burning my lips
rounding the tops of knees.

its been new looking out the window with the
        screen pulled back
sticking my neck faaar

been listening,
what i speak with now
are these new moons keep me up
        remembering well

what i speak with now are the melodies
growing when they get time
sun beaming down from the skies
shining on all these places cause ain't no time
        to hide!

and

one moon

if secrets tear people apart then telling the truth
    must keep them together
and he told the truth
that he wasn't ready
that his tide couldn't rise quite yet
that his seasons weren't so seasonal and i was
    coming looking for spring in fall.

mute. left me mute.
with nothing running through, no thoughts,
    words, blank pages, writer's block.
speakers caught off.
caught with the guard having already put his
    swords down
couldn't really talk, could only really look in the
    other direction

so i didn't feel togetha
thought we had laid down this path to walk on,
we was walking along
too long, too short
either way you couldn't hang.
sorry if that was unfair, it's, you said you could
    just not quite anything,
just
eitherwayweshouldmakesurewe'refriendscause
    wegottaslooowthingsdooownandyou'renot
    surehowitwillturnoutnowsoweshouldbe
clear:
either way
either way
either way.
speaking honestly is respectful...

honestly? you crept up on me with that speech
cause we was laying down patchwork quilts to be
    warm in these chicago winters and i didn't
    care if spring was gonna come cause i was
    ready for some kind journey
...i guess either way.
we was runnin, and not that there is any type of
    finish line or any need to get ta one
we was runnin and wasn't outta breath and
    outta somewhere,
how do you not know how fast you need to go
    once you start?
maybe because there is no pace in matters
    of the mind
it's just try it until you get it right next time.

to be clear, in what you said you needed there
        was nothing i objected to.
speaking honestly is respectful: and this way,
        i was feelin the blues
didn't feeeel togetha.
thought,
it's gotta be the weather.
realized,
it's gotta be nothing, cause once it's gotta be
        sumthin it can't be what its gonna be
        naturally
gotta fly gotta be free,
gonna be okay,
either way

in recognition of now's truth

it may just be
that what I was seein'
only existed inside
my own head
i may have seen the sun when it
        was rainin'
or built a sandcastle
in the midst
of a windstorm
but you can't really
apologize
for luvin' somebody
only thing to do is
paddle with the current
instead of against it
'til I get my strength
back
lay down lonesomeness
and share it
remberin' the good things
like
at least I tried

        – cheryl johnson-odim,
        "other women before me"

H.is I.s P.lenty, H.ow O.urs P.ours

él me cae bien, como el sol le cae al mar
sin los "comos"...
él es un árbol con hojas muchas
yo, un tambor
mi pecho imitando el sonido
palpitando
nosotros dos paseos llegando dónde llegamos
sin querer, sin queridos
somos amigos nuevos
encontrando el fondo, llegando dónde llegamos.
a ti llego con mis ojos abiertos
escuchando a tus talones que me guían
exactamente como el sonido saltando del tambor
saliendo de mi tambor
buscándote
con tu mano en mi mano te encuentro.
guardando las piedras y las maderas
y los sentidos, tu me puedas guardar también?
a ti yo llego con preguntas, muchas
las que pueden llenar el mar,
y cuando te llego, las dejo
porque aquí veo que las debo dejar.

maple sugar boy*

our light trembled in the sky too soon.
dripping, melting
till there is no more.

and into the bottom of this box i stay looking
thinking of its appearing self
right there right there in the shadows!

those boats not by the water, keeping me thirsty
drinking water to no avail
round about in circles my body turns and wails

*title borrowed from the song, maple sugar boy
(buffy sainte-marie, album: many a mile)

don't get it twisted

i've treated love like a poem i'd write:
you leave a poem and it's there for you,
it actually grows in your absence, sometimes
needs your absence to grow;
needs you to come back to it so it can be written.
you leave a love,
and they just leave you. no coming back
...don't get it twisted.

just write

"Sometimes I can just write fast from the heart
until I'm healed."

– Patricia J. Williams

traveling staffs

dee jay

beat said:
all
and only soul
light in and full
wants noise
the fire
and time
long
fast
or wild.

would they group
naked at microphone
after some music?

rhythm say so.
have it hit
beneath life
...almost anthem, but right.

bass going:
do make
to move, do make –to move
sweetest as song

te

I

¡aquí estamos y no nos vamos!
aquí estamos y nos vamos pushing up with bent
      elbows
rising like steam from tea
hanging heavy in the air
hitting pitch and smooooooth
riding out,
wave length ring

i mean this assortment of all of us
weight sharing, sometimes tipping.

one time, a friend looking exactly like herself
sent me her thoughts
her words breaking open meanings:
telling of how we are a part of her share me vision
apart of being who we are: who are we?
doing and going
banking on it...secrets don't reside here
got me thinking my people
got me believing:
i
am my own
hot, sticky
thick, heavy, meaty you have trouble biting
      through it foundation

mi gente
got me thinking
you don't have to know the pain to feel the hurt
      sometimes
you don't have to know the dance steps to enjoy
      the movement

II

double dutch is movement
bachata is smile
suya is spice and salsa is this point from which
    hips pivot

III

rise pivoting hips
bending limbs
hitting pitches in chunk

for

we are not finished
we are writers of our history while living the
    present
breathing the past, exhaling right now
lean in
on whatever or how ever you call it
land
whenever how ever you call it
late night, madrugada
however long
four weeks, one moon
speak it on the wind so it carries
holds heavy in air
saturates light
shows the exact shade you see

go tell it on the mountain

uplift whatcha think
can't lift no one else till ya uplift yaself
then bring it home

bring it to what home is for you...don't always
        have to go down first to come up
cause when we water,
life thanks the spirits who bring
gracious movement here
handling la tierra
reaching the skies
bending backs
stretching spines
being with ourselves
knowing my life is life enough to share it with
        myself
it's big enough for the souls of me and stretches
        with the we

v
our sea salts let's not dissolve into water
our bodies lets keep moving in different
        directions
our body minds, when seated rest on thought
move on action when we collide

beauty

how did we get started with all these festivities?
people have been decorating themselves for
        centuries but not like this...
with all the tucked in changes
        and the rearranges
just let it fall like it did when u were born baby!

we have to decorate it, but keep it loved
cause we are what it is just as you are how you is,
beautiful.
you knew this tho, that's why you care about
        your beautiful
the thing is you don't need to put anything in
        to do it tho
just get up in the morning with some soap and
        water and do it yo
fluid.
cause too much fussin' and fighting' will trash it
we are not elastic
and deff not plastic
so this that we are supposed to look like...
        pass that
if we move together we can move past this.

it's not about putting up new images cause that
        is the bad ish,
it's about not needing billboards and adver-
        tisements and magazines to look at like,
        "that's it!"

if you know what you're doing,
        then be what you need.
go tell it on your mountains and let your words
        breathe:

we are this earth!
as earth is air!
as fire is water!
as day is night!
we are affected by what is out there,
        this affecting how it shines inside our light!

this, this right here, this heart
this is it
we make our pathways,
(these histories we leave behind showing
        what we do)
this journey is continuous
our eyes, map these landscapes. sueños, dreams,
        these threads we quilt our lives with
gotta keep quilting, gotta keep quilting
gotta keep our minds right!

you see it's about feeling,
        and that needed feeling
comes from the groove that sits in your hips
comes from the pictures you make with
        your wrists,
(the writing, the movement and colors all of it)
comes from your beauty and how you choose
        to decorate this

cop cars

cop cars creep curiously
cops come carrying crank
crack!
chest
clank clank,
creep creep...

WHAT TIME IS IT? NATION TIME!
WHAT'S GONNA' HAPPEN?
LANDS GONNA' CHANGE HANDS!

WHAT TIME IS IT?
NATION TIME!
WHAT'S GONNA' HAPPEN?
LANDSGONNA'CHANGE HANDS!
WHATTIMEISIT?NATIONTIME!WH
AT'SGONNA'HAPPEN?LANDSGON
NA'CHANGEHANDS!

who's gonna do it?
probably those here to see the land taken in the
        first place

those figuring

whose words
strangled
chewed up,
spit out by manifest destiny
mass graves dug by museums, dissected by
        anthropology
buried by so called saviors
these overseers who attack and
rest
attempt to do for those they infect
attempt to do for their children too
and their children's children too...

will be here

the people,
the humans across the earth shall march
inspired not by revenge but by avenging the slow
    killings,
not having to be oppressed to uprise*

the people, the humans
across the earth
those whose midday mush was seasoned with the
    spices of flying away
whose hair was weaving leaving family
and liberating self
whose vocal chords stretch(ed) with the
    exercises of
negro spirituals
ellas y ellos hicieron una promesa solemne:
    sobrevivir

with feet marching now, legacies coming to
    travel
and those resting making their ways through

tomando las manos de ellas y ellos
los y las, quienes lenguas extranjeros trataron
    de robar
vendrán
levantando

es el tiempo del nación y las tierras cambiaran
    manos!

with voice
with feet
with vibrating land...

tomando sus manos
vendramos vendramos
traveling on mother earth's land
re-establishing our nations
spread out, breaking state lines across the earth

nation time!

those coming who witnessed those who marched.
(mouths moving simultaneously)
those who marched having witnessed those
        defeniendo las fronteras
who witnessed:
those drawing nutrition from voice
drawing strength from down winds
and strength from
the tactics
of
those fighting against colón-ization
(and those mother earth cradles)
        con manos arriba

with hands in the air
we will come running
the globe.
watches on our wrists
asking,
what time is it?

nation time!
what's gonna' happen?
lands gonna' change hands!

*quote from a professor

i have been the bloody revolution
carrying buckets full, laughing so politely to the
      kitchen to fix up massa's food
real well and good
to the kitchen mammy!
a la cocina!
wolf killer in the middle of the oysters,
don't want no scraps today massa! no sir!

been the bloody revolution
because i'd rather wash the blood off my hands
      than place my little girl in the hands of hat
      plantation
been the spinal chords bending overboard on
      ships cause i'd rather be in her belly than
      give my sons
to whips
been eyes sparkling in the reflection of star's
      light, with pepper on her heals and a pair
      of wings to fly, been birds
rising
as high as i can see, past the mountain we tell it
      on,
going towards home.
been the seated and the marching
the gathering and the making
i be
my -ness redefining return
i am my colors, my white bones, my eyes, my
      fathers and my mothers

redefining return

washing in the river and forgetting everything except – water
    grows.
she said,
and history is how the secular world attends to the dead
    –Hartman
heartstrings
are taut to walk on to cross the Atlantic the other way,
walking now chained to the longing
walking now chained to the playing field
only leveling my chances of physical pain.
still
beating my brains and whipping my spirit,
holding it up by its ankles and raping its birth.
tarnishing and tarring my memory even after you've taken me
beating my bloods blue with your stride for nobility

the hide, the pen
the chain, the want
the blood, the sweat of manual labor and juegos de baloncesto
of soaking red and blue bandanas
the auction block the police issued hand gun
the ocean, the land
returning?
on journey the other way can't only be defined as literal
        movement,
has to be: growing yams in ears.
drying fish for the walk back from the coast
drying fish 'cause not just the coast gets fish,
wrapping cloth, patterned life
wrapping cloth, thinking of what an American identity is
where do i actually belong, question mark.

the whole country has to think you are American
our whole country has to think about these identities
the whole country has to think i will not tell you how your
        movements move
our whole country has to think, greeting me – every time i come
        home telling of the igbo name i have to be greeted by.
the whole country has to think about losing your mother
and caged birds
and knowing your mother but not knowing how her cheeks smell
and caged birds,
and knowing good food
and finding cage doors
and knowing that not only black birds are caged
get it?
and knowing that not only black bodies are in those cages, get it?

what do we see in you
i see, there is nothing to have to make up for not having the
     cuartos
or the monedas, the rose shit that isn't really shit
     cause it doesn't smell
there is nothing to have that needs to make up for what you think
     i am unfortunate enough for not having

redefining my return

this one race – human race thought
i don't mean like that
this, wear a ring – put a ring on it talk
don't call me it
i'm meaning ring out that cloth soaked with define IT
ring out that heavy cloth
ring out that cloth sweated in.

56

for the mine that is only ours,
for the voice i speak with that is only mine

she said,
i been to sorrow's kitchen and licked out all the pots- Straight
across the brims
the ones holding cafesitos, habichuelas con dulce
ropas viejas, flan y mate son dulces

been to sorrow's kitchen and looked him straight between the
        eyes
and they said
break
and i said, can't/won't
and they say
paint you nails long, wear your heels high

splash your face with pro-actively created make up
        your self better
feeeeeeel better!
and i say, doesn't feeeeeeel better
and they say
don't look to your people,
cassavas, turmerics, saffrons,
look to the standard
and i say
look to my people
and my people aren't only black get it?

tierra biafra

i imagine covering my face with a million ribbons of straw
red beads around my eyes
suya spice on my teeth
air on my mouth
mask
with
red grains of jolof rice, sweet sugar from chin-chin
open palms facing my forehead is how i will place it.

on my head i have cloth
wrapping around my thoughts with turquoise swirl burgundy eye
      drop patterns on top of tan warmth
      impregnated with thought giving birth,
date seeds in my pockets.
kola nuts are bitter and so good like all the palm offerings
      i embrace
like light shining in nigeria
ni-ge-ri-a
just like that, in the morning like that.

let me cut my hair down low
don't ask me how or when it grows
don't finger it.

abiriba thinks
igbo woman body is beautiful, soft and sweet smelling good
with bent joints
elbows and knees
not only feet but hands too
not perfect, makes mistakes too
that's how abiriba walks
bendin her back like it's goin outta style

peace

composed of these intricate little
branches
lining themselves up like steps of our existence,
deep
and smelling good to the soul
round, circular, heavy weighted, colorful.
sure footed
and able to balance,
to reach,
to have wing spans
plural
amounts and mounds in bellies filling
so we can fly!
to stay alive.
a tener en nuestro paseo
aquí dentro, dentro
al fondo
reaching to the tips of toes
reaching to the tips of fingers
spreading to the backs of heads

and out, and out the eyes.
seeing the sea's blues and remembering old man
        river's belly,
sometimes waking at night with the sorrow of
        indigestion
the stomach
in the middle passage
of thought:
the deep deep, down by the river's deep
where the peaceful keep
bellas, por que los espiritus se hacen así

a daughter of daughters of sons

this sapphire, this moon
tip toeing at sky's edge and chasing the sun
along it
beside it

                                a long way home

i am maya emma nnena ruth odim. a daughter, younger sister, cousin, aunt, niece and granddaughter. poetry has been a part of my life since i can remember learning how to write words. all thanks i'm giving to family and friends for chilling, teaching, sharing, keeping me living in the now and working to be peaceful.

"Keep your eyes on the prize." – mom

"As you change, the world changes with you." – dad

i have experience facilitating poetry/spoken word and creative writing workshops in various spaces in illinois as well as connecticut, and share/perform poetry regularly.